DATES IN THE STATES

A COUPLE TRAVELING THE UNITED
STATES ON A BUDGET

Mystery Date
Canandaigua, NY

By Dates in the States

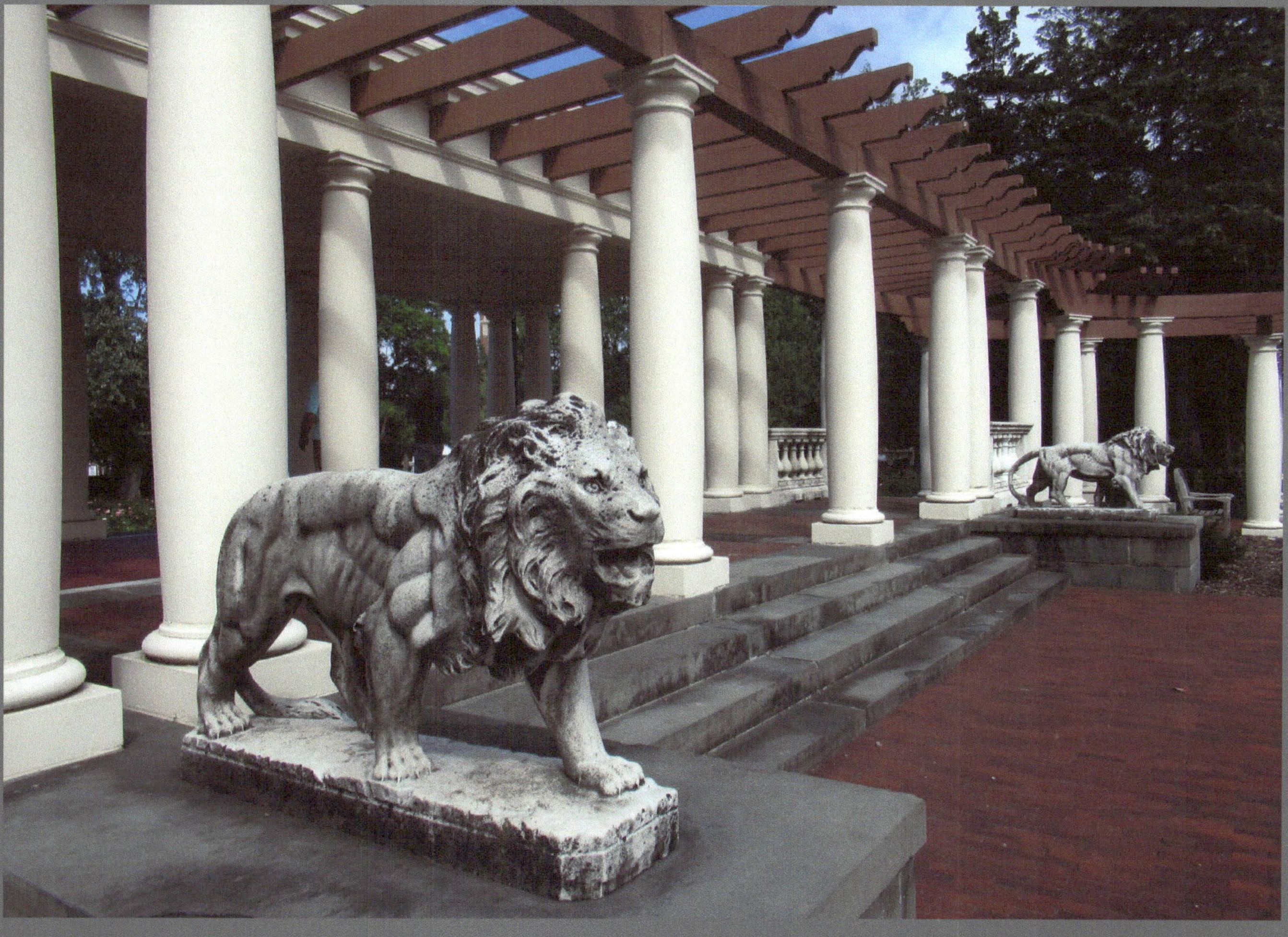

"Our passion is travel, and we want to share our adventures to inspire others to explore the world with their loved ones. Dare to live beyond the box."

Dates in the States

Introduction

Hey there! We're Crystal and Shane, the duo behind Dates in the States, where we share our love for discovering unique adventures, unforgettable moments, and hidden gems across the U.S. Whether you're searching for a fun date idea, a new place to explore, or just a little inspiration, we've got you covered!

Our Mystery Date Books are designed to help couples (and adventurous friends!) shake up their routine and experience the best local spots in a fun, intentional way. Inside, you'll find a curated collection of date ideas—each one meant to be completed over the course of a single day in a specific neighborhood. All of which are a surprise until you flip the page!

We hope this book helps you laugh more, explore more, and connect more—with each other and with your city. Let the mystery begin!

Here's What To Expect:

This Canandaigua Mystery Date Book is your guide to one of our favorite small-town escapes in the Finger Lakes. Whether you're planning a day date or just looking for something different to do, we've mapped out a fun, easy-to-follow experience that shows off some of the best local spots.

You'll hit a mix of outdoorsy views, good food, and low-key places with a lot of character—no big chains, no fluff, just the kind of stops that make a place memorable. We kept it simple, intentional, and full of the stuff we'd want to do on a date ourselves.

No need to overthink it—just follow along, take it one stop at a time, and enjoy the day.

First Stop

Simply Crêpes
101 S Main St,
Canandaigua, NY 14424

Start your day with a hearty meal at Simply Crêpes, a cozy and charming eatery known for its creative menu and welcoming atmosphere. Located in the heart of Canandaigua, this family-owned spot is a local favorite and perfect for a leisurely breakfast or lunch. Their menu features both sweet and savory crêpes, with options to suit any craving. Our favorites are their savory crepes like the one pictured here stuffed with eggs and bacon!

If you're in the mood for something comforting, their chai latte is a standout, perfectly spiced and wonderfully creamy. The rustic décor and warm ambiance make it an ideal spot to fuel up before your adventures at Sonnenberg. Don't forget to ask about their seasonal specials for a unique twist on their classic offerings.

2nd Stop

Sonnenberg Gardens & Mansion

250 Gibson St,
Canandaigua, NY 14424

Built-in the late 1800s as a summer retreat, Sonnenberg features a magnificent 40-room mansion and nine historic gardens across 50 stunning acres. Begin your visit by touring the grounds and immersing yourself in the lush gardens, fountains, and floral displays. Be sure to explore the mansion and speak to guides who can offer fascinating insights and share personal anecdotes that are otherwise unheard of.

Before you leave, don't forget to stroll through the greenhouses, shop the plants they may have available and stop by the gift shop to browse their selection of local wines and unique, locally made goodies—a perfect way to remember your visit or find a thoughtful gift.

3rd Stop

Stroll Along Main Street

After your time at Sonnenberg, take a leisurely stroll along Canandaigua's picturesque Main Street, lined with charming boutiques and unique shops. Take your time exploring the shelves at Renaissance Goodie II Shoppe and Finger Lakes Treasure Trove, where you'll find everything from antiques to locally made treasures.

As you wander, pop into the many other delightful boutiques, thrift stores, and antique shops that line the street—you never know what you may find! Stop by Good Life Tea, our favorite spot to grab some samples and loose-leaf tea to make at home.

Fourth Stop
Rheinblick German Restaurant
224 S. Main St.
Canandaigua, NY 14424

End your date on a cozy and flavorful note with dinner at Rheinblick German Restaurant, a hidden gem that brings a taste of Bavaria to the heart of Canandaigua. Nestled just off Main Street, this family-owned spot is known for its warm hospitality, authentic German cuisine, and charming, old-world ambiance.

Share a giant pretzel with beer cheese, dive into traditional dishes like schnitzel or bratwurst, and raise a glass of German beer or Riesling to a date well done.

Whether you're seated indoors in their rustic dining room or enjoying the patio when the weather's nice, Rheinblick is the perfect spot to slow down, savor the flavors, and toast to the adventure you just shared.

Final Stop
Kershaw Park
155 Lakeshore Dr
Canandaigua, NY 14424

If the weather's nice, end your date at Kershaw Park to take in the lake views of Canandaigua. Parking is around $5, and it's totally worth it.

We almost always try to take a walk after we eat, and this is one of our favorite spots to do just that—relaxing, scenic, and the perfect way to wind down the day. In the summer, we love watching the boats come and go from the marina, and there's usually a good mix of people out enjoying the park.

The cold months are quieter, but still a great spot for a brisk walk—most of the paved paths are maintained, and the lake views are just as beautiful.

Add Your Photos

Keepsakes

Thank you for joining us on this mystery date adventure! We hope you've enjoyed the delightful experiences and memorable moments we've crafted just for you in Canandaigua, NY.

But the adventure doesn't stop here! Keep exploring exciting myster dates in other cities and uncover new romantic experiences across the U.S. by visiting our website, DatesInTheStates.com. There, you can purchase both physical copies and digital downloads of our mystery date books. Plus, don't miss out on our Mystery Date Book Club, where you can receive a brand-new mystery date book every month!

Tag us in your date photos on social media! @datesinthestates

Check out some of our other Mystery Date Books:

Webster, NY – Lakeside charm, local eats, and small-town surprises perfect for a relaxing day out.

Haunted Irondequoit, NY – Explore the eerie side of town with this chilling look into the most haunted businesses and their spine-tingling stories.

Hornell, NY – A hidden gem in the Finger Lakes region with art, nature, and charming local spots waiting to be discovered.

I Love ROC + Cats – Explore local art, sip coffee with adoptable cats, browse a charming bookstore, and end with a delicious downtown meal. Perfect for solo dates, friend hangouts, or cat-loving couples!

✉ Shop them all at DatesInTheStates.com

📷 Tag your adventures: @datesinthestates

Your next date is only a page away.

About the Creators

Crystal, the writer and creator, is a storyteller at heart. When she's not uncovering hidden gems for the next date night idea, she runs her own digital marketing company, helping small businesses improve their content marketing, increase visibility in their communities, and streamline their online presence.
Visit: crystalstatskey.com

Shane, her husband and partner in adventure, is a dedicated personal trainer and the owner of Beekstar Fitness in Irondequoit, NY. He specializes in working with clients who have limited mobility, helping them build muscle and focus on pain areas so they can regain strength and confidence in their daily lives.
Visit: beekstarfitness.com

Crystal and Shane have explored every U.S. state except Alaska (coming soon!) and are now visiting countries in alphabetical order. Whether road-tripping or curating Mystery Date experiences, they're always chasing their next adventure.

Local Love

A few local gems in Canandaigua
worth exploring on your next date.

NEW YORK KITCHEN
COOKING CLASSES AND EVENTS
800 S MAIN ST, CANANDAIGUA, NY 14424

TWISTED RAIL BREWING
LAID-BACK BREWERY WITH CRAFT BEERS
169 LAKESHORE DR, CANANDAIGUA, NY 14424

SWEET EXPRESSIONS
DELICIOUS FUDGE & SWEETS
169 S MAIN ST, CANANDAIGUA, NY 14424

Want to see your business here?
See the next page for details on
how to join!

Want to be featured?

MYSTERY DATE BOOK PACKAGES

—

Are you a small business looking to reach new customers? Feature your business in our next Mystery Date Book! Choose from our partnership packages below to connect with couples seeking unique experiences and exclusive deals.

Package One

LOCAL LOVE LISTING

—

A quick shoutout to show you're part of the neighborhood vibe.

Listed in the "Local Love" section of your designated neighborhood date book

Includes business name, address, and social link

Optional: Offer a small promo (e.g., 10% off for book holders)

1 social media shout-out when the book launches

$45

Package Two

FEATURE STOP

—

You're not just a business— you're part of the experience.

Marked as a "Must-Stop" on a Mystery Date

Full-page feature in the book with your story, offerings and photo

Includes 1 social media feature — a dedicated post and story highlighting your business

Note: To ensure each feature is genuine and experience-based, we require a hosted visit prior to inclusion.

$95

Package Three

PARTNER & SELLER

—

Be the spot and the source.

Everything in Tier 2

PLUS: Option to sell the Mystery Date Books at your location

Includes a bulk purchase of 10 books (yours to price + sell)

Keep 100% of the profits from in-store sales

Bonus: Tag as an official pickup location in our promotions

$150

Prices are subject to change

Feel free to reach us at any time by sending us an email to say hi and to learn more! We look forward to hearing from you.

| www.datesinthestates.com | datesinthestatesblog@gmail.com |

Sponsors & Affiliates

Our sponsors and affiliates help make our adventures possible! Explore the amazing brands and businesses that support our community.

Wanderful

Wanderful is a global community for women who love to travel. Connect, explore, and join a local hub near you!

Join our Book Club!

Join our Mystery Date Book Club and be part of a travel-inspired community, discovering unique local adventures together!

HomeExchange

HomeExchange lets you swap homes with travelers worldwide for authentic, affordable stays. Join today and travel differently!

Shop our books at a store near you!

Little Button Craft
658 South Ave.
Rochester, NY 14620

The Pawsitive Cat Cafe
120 East Ave. Ste 100
Rochester, NY 14604

Yesterday's Muse Books
32 West Main St.
Webster, NY 14580

Writers & Books
740 University Ave,
Rochester, NY 14607

Littleberger Florist
63 North Avenue,
Webster, NY 14580

Abundance Food Co-op
571 South Ave,
Rochester, NY 14620

Scents by Design
728 University Ave,
Rochester, NY 14607

Union Tavern
4565 Culver Rd,
Irondequoit, NY 14622

DATES IN THE STATES

A COUPLE TRAVELING THE UNITED
STATES ON A BUDGET

Contact Us

datesinthestates.com

✉

datesinthestatesblog@gmail.com

📍

Based in Rochester, NY

CONNECT WITH US ON SOCIAL!

@DATESINTHESTATES

_____